Pure aı

How to Simplify Your Life, Do Less, and Get More

By Martin Meadows

Download another Book for Free

I want to thank you for buying my book and offer you another book (just as long and valuable as this book), *Grit: How to Keep Going When You Want to Give Up*, completely free.

Visit the link below to receive it:

http://www.profoundselfimprovement.com/pureandsimple

In *Grit*, I'll share with you exactly how to stick to your goals according to peak performers and science.

In addition to getting *Grit*, you'll also have an opportunity to get my new books for free, enter giveaways, and receive other valuable emails from me.

Again, here's the link to sign up:

http://www.profoundselfimprovement.com/pureandsimple

Table of Contents

Prologue

When I heard about the 80/20 Principle for the first time (from Richard Koch's book *The 80/20 Principle*[i]), I didn't fully understand its implications. The most common example was: "80% of your profits come from 20% of your clients." That was easy enough, but didn't sound practical for everyday use except for business.

It took me a few years to grasp the full meaning and impact of this rule and the power of simplification implemented on a daily basis.

Simplification started making more sense each time I cut away the unessential and got better results while doing less. Soon, I made it my number one rule in life.

This book won't explain in detail the 80/20 Principle or its implications in business. We won't discuss statistics or talk about theory.

Instead, the goal of this book is to help you escape the trap of complexity by learning how to focus on the vital few instead of the trivial many. I'll show you why you should trim away the "fat" in your life and how to do it.

Once you finish the book, you'll have a better idea how to reduce or eliminate the activities that don't bring value in your life. You'll be able to enjoy the simplicity and, most importantly, stick to it instead of defaulting to complexity once again.

Just like maintaining a healthy weight requires healthy habits, living a simplified life requires maintaining a few simple habits, too. You'll discover the most important question to ask yourself each time you want to add something in your life. You'll also increase your life satisfaction by making a simple switch in your priorities and acquire a powerful skill for virtually unlimited achievement.

As in my every book, I point to numerous resources and scientific research to base the advice and claims on something more than just my subjective opinion. However, the book – as every book in this genre – is still based primarily on my views and ideas which you may or may not agree with. My goal is to help you reconsider how you live your life, not tell you how you should live it, as the answer varies for each person.

Each chapter ends with a quick recap to help you review it. If you're after getting the most knowledge in as little time as possible, you don't need to read the entire book. 80% of its value will be found in these short chapter summaries. If, however, you want to have a more enjoyable reading experience, I invite you to follow me through every single chapter.

Chapter 1: The Power of Fewer Choices

Let's start with a quick exercise. Please come up with a general outline for a short story in your mind. It can be about anything you want. Nothing constraints you. Who are the characters? What do they do? What's the conflict?

How difficult do you find it to come up with something on the spot?

Now come up with a short romance story taking place in a small town between a local doctor and his patient.

How difficult was it to come up with a quick storyline with these constraints?

I bet you could imagine a scene between the doctor and the patient right away.

That's the power of exclusion and constraint. Logic says you'll be more creative if I tell you that you can come up with anything you want. Yet, it's when I limit your choices you become more imaginative.

Constraints not only make you more creative, they also help you make better decisions that will leave you more satisfied.

In a famous study conducted by Sheena Iyengar from Columbia University and Mark Lepper from Stanford University, participants who were offered 24 or 30 choices of jams were ten times less likely to make a purchase than the participants who were offered a choice of 6 jams[ii]. Moreover, participants were more satisfied with their selections when they had a limited set of options.

Their findings don't only apply to choosing between different jams. Fewer choices in general dramatically reduce the complexity in our everyday lives and make the final choice more satisfying.

A study on the number of product capabilities conducted by the researchers from the University of Maryland[iii] shows that overly complex products lead to "feature fatigue," which reduces the user's satisfaction.

The results of the study show that companies should offer a large number of specialized products instead of one product with an overwhelming number of features (if you have ever used customer management software, you can probably relate to that).

The availability of endless options should give us more freedom. Usually it's the other way around. Trying to choose between numerous options causes unnecessary stress and unhappiness.

Analysis paralysis, the state of over-analyzing a situation, permeates every single aspect of our lives – if we don't know how to deal with it.

Sheena Iyengar and her colleagues conducted another experiment on the harmful effect of too many choices. The team of researchers discovered that employee participation in 401(k) plans fell as the number of fund options was increased[iv]. When there were only two choices, 75% of employees participated. When they were offered 59 options, 61% of employees participated.

I too suffered from a similar problem. When I was looking for a simple savings account offering the best interest rate, I had to compare more than just interest rates. Most offers came with numerous stipulations, making it extremely hard to compare different options. It would take hours just to check every offer, and I would still second-guess my choice afterwards.

In the end, I went with the simplest offer with a lower interest but with no additional provisions. I greatly limited my choice by skipping bank offers with numerous stipulations, and consequently made my choice much easier.

Now that you've discovered how too many choices affect your life negatively, there's a clear path you can consider taking – living your life in such a way that your options are always reduced to the most viable ones.

Each area of life comes with different challenges to reduce the number of choices. In the remaining part of this chapter, we'll go through some of the most important areas of your life and ways to reduce the number of choices.

Everyday Life

In my book *How to Build Self-Discipline: Resist Temptations and Reach Your Long-Term Goals*, I mentioned a story of President Obama, who once said in an interview, "You'll see I wear only gray or blue suits. I'm trying to pare down decisions. I don't want to make decisions about what I'm eating or wearing. Because I have too many other decisions to make"[v].

Other people who have been known for wearing the same clothes include Facebook's co-founder Mark Zuckerberg (a gray t-shirt with a black hoody and jeans), Steve Jobs (black turtleneck and jeans), and Albert Einstein (a gray suit)[vi]. All of these people decided that the energy spent making a frivolous decision in the morning wasn't worth it.

While limiting your clothing choices to improve the quality of your life sounds ridiculous, even such small changes can simplify your day. When was the last time you cleaned your wardrobe and got rid of the things you no longer wear? How often do you spend more than five to ten minutes choosing your outfit?

Cleaning your closet will not only benefit you, but also other people to whom you can sell or give the clothes you no longer wear.

I own very few clothes because I don't get enjoyment out of spending hours choosing the perfect outfit. If it gives you enjoyment, don't give up on it (simplifying your life doesn't mean becoming ascetic), but find a way to get rid of the clothes you never wear anyway.

If you're considering wearing the same set of clothes every day, but you're worried people will criticize you or make fun of you, don't worry. Australian TV anchor Karl Stefanovic wore the same blue suit every day for a year. Nobody noticed anything[vii]. I'm pretty sure that on any given day there were many more eyeballs on him than on you.

The second part of Obama's quote, about decisions regarding what he's eating, leads to another piece of advice to consider – simplifying your meals so that you always have a few staple meals to choose from.

A lot of reluctance to cook at home comes from the fact that it's difficult to come up with a recipe and cook a perfect dinner. What if you mastered preparing just a few staple meals so you could always cook them in 15 minutes or less? Wouldn't it dramatically reduce your temptation to grab an unhealthy candy bar or hamburger and wash it down with a cup of highly-caloric iced coffee or soft drink?

My diet consists primarily of a few staple, easy to cook meals. It doesn't mean I don't draw any enjoyment out of eating. Despite having the same meals over and over, I still feel satisfied (and I still eat different things from time to time).

By simplifying what I eat, I have more "decision making power" left for other things I find more important in my life. While my choice is extreme to some people, and I don't try to convert anyone to a bland diet, it serves me well.

You can follow the same approach in your everyday life by reducing the number of choices regarding things that aren't important to you. For me, spending time trying to come up with a perfect outfit or a meal is not worth it. For you, choosing between numerous outfits can be a highly-rewarding activity you should continue doing.

Another simple way to reduce the number of choices in your everyday life is to develop a morning routine and follow it every single day. I've already covered this in detail in my book, *How to Relax: Stop Being Busy, Take a Break, and Get Better Results While Doing Less.*

If you know exactly how your day will start, you'll enjoy much calmer mornings. You won't have to spend time figuring out whether you should eat or take a shower first, check your email or meditate, write down an entry in your gratitude journal or go for a walk. Your routine will free you to spend your time thinking about other things.

Which other aspects of your life can you simplify so you don't have to waste your energy making the choice?

Fitness and Health

There are hundreds (if not thousands) of diets to choose from. The same can be said about different exercises and workouts that are "proven" to help you lose weight or build muscle. In all these cases, the overwhelming number of choices only leads to analysis paralysis which makes us unable to choose anything.

In the ancient fable *The Fox and the Cat*, a cat and a fox discuss how many tricks they have to escape the hunters. The fox boasts that he has many; the cat confesses to having only one. When hunters arrive with their dogs, the cat quickly climbs a tree, but the fox is caught by the hounds, unable to choose between his hundreds of tricks.

What's the point of knowing hundreds of diets if you can't stick with one? Why learn hundreds of exercises if you only need to perform a few of them to achieve your results?

I'm a big believer in extreme simplification in fitness and health. Strength training can be reduced to just three to five basic movements (the Big Three movements are: squat, deadlift and bench press; pull-ups/chin-ups and overhead press are two additional basic movements more advanced trainees can add to their workout)[viii].

You can spend hours looking for the perfect workout plan, or you can choose one of the simplest plans possible and stick to it for a year. A simpler plan should be enough to make you realize you have no need to learn other exercises.

As for health, I've already touched briefly upon the concept of eating the same meals over and over. It doesn't necessarily mean you have to eat a bland diet. Either preparing your meals in advance or eating the same (or similar) staple meals every single day will take the guesswork out of the equation. It will help you lose weight (or build muscle) much faster than when you're not sure what (and how much) to eat.

The temptation to eat the wrong kind of food is often the result of laziness. If your meals are already prepared (or you can prepare them quickly), you'll increase your chances of success.

Many people find it hard to engage in regular physical activity. Instead of following simple advice, they try to follow the latest "trendy" way of exercising. Pick one or two activities you enjoy the most and keep doing them instead of doing what you don't enjoy.

If working out at the gym is not your thing (and you don't have a goal of building muscle), go on a bike ride, learn how to dance, or climb rock walls. It doesn't matter what it is, as long as it helps you be active and you enjoy it.

Relationships

British anthropologist Robin Dunbar discovered[ix] that there's a cognitive limit to the number of people with whom we can maintain stable social relationships (by a stable relationship he means that you know who each person is and how she relates to every other person).

The number is 150. There are sublevels that exist within that circle. At the top there are the five people who are closest to you: your family and best friends. Then there are another ten more people, usually your relatives. You interact with your top 15 every week or so. The next 35 people are people with whom you meet on about a monthly basis. All the other relationships are people with whom you communicate from time to time, every few months or less often.

In his article for Institute of Electrical and Electronics Engineers, Dunbar says: "Data that my colleagues at the University of Oxford and I have gathered suggest that if you start to invest less time in a friendship, the emotional quality of the relationship will decay within at most six months. The relationship will gradually bump its way down through the layers of friendship until eventually it slips over the weir [sic] at 150 and that person becomes "one of those people I once knew""[x].

The more friends you have, the more difficult it is to keep up with them. Consequently, your friendships will decay.

The high number of social choices harms your social life instead of enriching it. All these different invitations to hang out on the same day with different people are standing in your way toward enjoyment and satisfaction with the few, key individuals in your life.

Solution? Carefully select your closest friends and understand that the more people you let into your closest circle, the more difficult it will be to maintain high-quality relationships with them.

Money and Business

Whether you're working a regular job, are a freelancer, or a business owner, the same rules apply – if you don't have clearly defined skills, you'll struggle making money. People who dig deep instead of digging dozens of holes are the ones we consider experts and the ones whose advice, services or products we value the most.

These are the people who spend hundreds of hours learning the ins and outs of an industry to become the go-to person.

These are the authors like Stephen King, who has been consistently writing 2,000 words a day ever since he started[xi]. He spends the majority of his time on reading and writing, the two single most important activities for a writer.

These are entrepreneurs like Richard Branson, who focuses on starting new businesses, but not managing them (you can do many things, as long as they all have something specific in common).

As Branson said in an article for Entrepreneur.com[xii], "Looking back, my decision to work out of my houseboat in West London rather than at Virgin Records' offices was a very important move. This happened about the same time I split Virgin Records into two. I decided to take a step back to give my managers space to make decisions. That's when I learned that the most successful entrepreneurs are those who find people who are at least as good as, or better than, they are at running their businesses."

The more activities you do, the more slowly you grow and the longer you have to practice until you become a master at something. The vast number of career or business choices you can make doesn't mean you should make them. For most of us, it's a sure-fire path to being mediocre in several things instead of being great at one thing.

What is your number one ability? Do you spend the majority of your time doing it, or do you jump from one thing to another?

THE POWER OF FEWER CHOICES: QUICK RECAP

1. Limiting your choices helps you make a decision and enjoy it more than if you were offered numerous options to choose from.

2. If you're faced with too many choices, there's a high risk you'll suffer from paralysis analysis, a condition that makes you unable to choose any option. The main way of dealing with this problem is to reduce the number of available options.

3. Consider simplifying your everyday life by reducing the number of unimportant decisions such as choosing the right outfit (by limiting the number of clothes), meal (by eating the same or similar meals), and what to do in the morning (by sticking to a morning routine).

4. Many problems with health and fitness are the result of too many choices. Find the simplest possible way to lose weight and/or become active, and stick to it. The more you know, the less likely you are to take any action.

5. The more friends you have, the easier it is to weaken each of your friendships. Focus on quality and think twice before you let anyone enter your inner circle of the five or so people closest to you.

6. In business and money, dig deep instead of digging hundreds of holes. Become an expert who possesses one unique skill instead of knowing many things at a mediocre level.

Chapter 2: What Really Makes You Happy

When you think about buying something that will make you happy, do you think of an item or an experience? If you've chosen the latter, you've made the right choice – at least according to positive psychology.

Psychology professors Thomas Gilovich, Matthew Killingsworth, and Cornell doctorate Amit Kumar suggest in their research paper[xiii] that spending money on experiences provides more enduring happiness than spending it on things. Specifically, the anticipation of experiential purchases is what's more pleasurable and exciting than waiting to receive a material good.

In another study, conducted by Thomas Gilovich and Leaf Van Boven[xiv], the researchers discovered that people think more often about past experiential purchases than the material ones.

It sounds rather obvious – we're more likely to reminisce about a great trip than a new smartphone bought a few years ago. However, when we dig deeper to understand the reasoning, we draw interesting conclusions.

In a subsequent research paper[xv], van Bowen suggested three reasons why experiences make us happier than material possessions.

1. Experiences improve with time; possessions do not.

You can reflect on a family summer trip to a national park in a much more abstract way than on a car. When you think about an experience, you bring up the associated feelings like the sun warming your skin on top of the mountain. You can't have the same experience when thinking about a car (you can think in this way about a road trip, though). A possession can rarely take on the same symbolic meaning in our memories.

2. Experiences are difficult to compare.

Each experience is unique. You can't say with absolute certainty that someone's trip was better than yours. However, you can compare cars and other possessions ("my car costs $20,000, his car costs $50,000, therefore I'm not happy with my car").

A study conducted by Sara J. Solnick and David Hemenway in 1998[xvi] uncovered a disturbing phenomenon. They found that people preferred to earn $50,000 a year while everyone else earned $25,000 instead of earning $100,000 themselves and other people earning $200,000.

I find it so disconcerting it's worth emphasizing – people were happier to make half as much money as long as others made less than them. Isn't it completely illogical? Wouldn't you want to make more, all things being equal? Yet, our human nature isn't always reasonable. We like to compare ourselves with others, even at our (great) expense.

That's why purchasing experiences rather than accumulating possessions results in a more satisfying life. You can't compare them easily, so you won't feel bad that someone had a "better" experience than you.

3. Experiences have a higher social value.

Experiences tend to benefit our relationships, thus making us happier. Moreover, it's socially acceptable to discuss our last trip to Hawaii with others, while talking about a new car sounds like boasting.

Despite all this research, an excessively materialistic lifestyle is still glorified in the mainstream media.

If you own an expensive, flashy car and live in a huge house (with rooms you haven't visited in years), you're someone (and you're certainly happy).

You absolutely have to buy this new expensive pair of shoes (even if you don't need them), because it's what "successful" people do.

If you buy this new smartphone (even if your current one is working perfectly), you'll be the coolest guy around.

But will you really?

What if instead of following the conventional mainstream "wisdom," you restructured your life to enrich it with experiences rather than possessions?

It's another part of your life you can greatly simplify to enjoy numerous benefits.

However, our ever useful brains sometimes come with a mechanism that makes us feel pain when we try to throw something out.

A Yale School of Medicine research on hoarders and non-hoarders[xvii] shows that hoarders confronted with throwing out their junk experienced conflict and pain. Yet, the mere presence of junk can also lead to conflict and pain. How do you solve this problem if you're one of these hoarders?

A study conducted by Sarah Bowen on college smokers who wanted to quit can help you[xviii]. In the study, one group of smokers was trained in a technique called "surfing the urge." When they felt a craving, they were asked to imagine the urge as a wave in the ocean – building in intensity, and eventually crashing and dissolving. Instead of fighting the wave, the smokers were asked to ride it – essentially being mindful[xix] about the experience. Another group didn't receive any training.

The group that received the training and followed the instructions was able to cut back smoking by 37%.

The same technique can be applied to fighting the urge to keep stuff you no longer need. Whenever you feel it, stay with the feeling without fighting it or giving in. When it passes (and it will, because delaying the urge until it fades away is the point of this exercise), you'll have an easier time decluttering your home.

3 Ways to Get Rid of Junk in Your Life

Clutter serves no purpose in your life. It takes up physical and mental space. It causes stress. It makes moving from one place to another a painful and time-consuming experience.

When you go through the ideas shared below and declutter your home, you too will realize how stuff has been holding you down. Then you will have an easier time moving on to a new way of life – a life that values experiences instead of things.

There are several main ways to get rid of physical junk from your life:

1. Get rid of the clothes you no longer wear

It's an obvious first step. Most people have wardrobes full of clothes they no longer wear. I used to keep things I hadn't worn in years, just because I thought I would wear them in the future. It didn't matter if they no longer fit me, had holes, or looked like it came from an 80's sitcom – I could still use them for something, right?

When I finally decided to get rid of the old clothes, my wardrobe went from a frightening, dark place to a refreshing place that stores only my most essential clothes. Now I rarely buy new clothes. I feel better having a small amount of high-quality clothes. Getting rid of the unnecessary clothes helped me:

- pack for trips. I don't need to spend hours thinking what to take with me. I only have the most essential clothes in my wardrobe.

- save time in the morning. If you only have a few pieces of classic clothing, you don't need to spend time choosing a perfect outfit.

- save money. By getting rid of unnecessary clothes, I learned which clothes I truly value – more expensive, high-quality pieces that will never go out of style. Now whenever I have to buy new clothes, I already know what I'm looking for.

Take inventory of your wardrobe, and get rid of any clothes you haven't worn in over a year. If you didn't need a piece of clothing in the last 12 months, you'll probably never need it (perhaps except for formal wear for weddings and other occasions).

2. Declutter the rest of your house

Each person has a different way of storing junk. Some people keep it in the attic. Others keep it in the basement or garage. Others have it spread all over their homes, tripping over it and complaining about it, though never taking action to get rid of it.

What's your style? Where do you keep most of your junk? I used to store a lot of my stuff on my desk.

By cleaning it, I decluttered my immediate work space. I instilled a rule to keep only the five to ten most essential items on my desk. I haven't looked back since – an empty desk makes me feel in control, while a cluttered one made me anxious.

However, for the sake of showing you a different perspective, it's worth noting that sometimes messy surroundings can be beneficial. A study conducted by Kathleen Vohs and her colleagues at the University of Minnesota[xx] shows that having an orderly room leads to healthier choices and generosity, while a disorderly room results in better creativity.

While an experiment on 48 people is not enough to draw any final conclusions, it suggests we can experiment with manipulating our state by either cleaning or cluttering our room. While I'm partial to simplicity and minimalism, it's a valuable experiment to test what works best for you.

If you have problems tossing stuff you no longer need because it has a sentimental value, move it to a different room for two weeks to trick your mind. If after two weeks you still feel strongly about throwing it away, keep it. If you realize its sentimental value is not worth the clutter it produces, get rid of it.

Keep in mind that simplifying your life is not about making yourself miserable for the sake of having fewer things. If you hold something dearly, don't throw it away – even if it's a collection of old vinyl records that takes a lot of space. It's about getting rid of things that suck the value out of your life (things you keep because "who knows, maybe I'll need them"), not mindlessly throwing away everything.

3. Declutter your digital life

If you're not living in a cave (and I'm pretty sure you aren't if you're reading this book), you probably spend a vast amount of your time on your laptop, smartphone, tablet, or other device. Your digital life is a huge part of your life, and it also needs decluttering. A simple act of clearing your desktop and browser of unnecessary items can lead to improved peace of mind.

I used to have dozens of icons on my desktop. It was annoying to search for what I needed, and it took up valuable time and energy. I got rid of all but the five most essential icons. As a result, I have a much easier time locating what I'm searching for. My desktop no longer makes me feel anxious that I have to clean it every single week.

Some people keep dozens of unread emails in their email account, marked as "to read later." Weeks pass, some emails are gone while new ones appear, and you never seem to reduce the total number of emails in the line.

Why not spend one evening going through all these emails to declutter your inbox? Once you're done, implement a new habit – you're never going to keep old emails unread for longer than 24-48 hours. A new routine is crucial here – if you don't come up with a way to prevent future cluttering, it will occur over and over again.

Moving from Things to Experiences

Once you identify and deal with the main culprits of clutter in your most immediate surroundings, you'll experience a newfound sense of calmness. Chaos around us tends to affect us in little ways we don't notice until we get rid of it. I know it affected me, and I've heard it countless times from other people who decided to declutter their lives.

As you get rid of unnecessary stuff, start filling your life with experiences – that's what's going to radically improve your well-being and happiness. Researchers from San Francisco State University[xxi] found that after making a purchase, the participants in the study were more satisfied with an experiential purchase than a material one.

Interestingly, the participants who were asked to prioritize happiness were more likely to pick a life experience, while participants prioritizing value were more likely to choose a material item. Most people know that experiences are better for their happiness, yet under normal circumstances, they still choose material items.

If you're overstressed, indulge by purchasing an experience, not a material item. A study on materialism conducted by Ayalla Ruvio and her colleagues[xxii] showed that compulsive and impulsive spending in the face of traumatic stress is likely to produce even greater stress and lower well-being.

Shopping can make things worse instead of better. There's no reason to buy stuff if you don't need it – it doesn't increase your happiness, nor is it useful. In reality, more often it will lead to mood shifts than real, lasting feelings of joy.

As Ed Diener, a University of Illinois psychology professor and happiness expert said, "those who value material success more than they value happiness are likely to experience almost as many negative moods as positive moods, whereas those who value happiness over material success are likely to experience considerably more pleasant moods and emotions than unpleasant moods and emotions"[xxiii].

Instead of living from one purchase to another, put happiness at the forefront of your mind. Analyze each of your major purchasing choices from the perspective of your long-term happiness rather than a short-term boost.

A new car will give you a positive feeling for a few days to a few weeks at most. A weeklong trip with your partner to Hawaii (or wherever you'd like to go) will give you joy for the rest of your life.

Moreover, a life focused on experiences will help you become more content with what you already have. While you can always crave more money, cars, clothes, a bigger house, a better yacht, etc. you don't usually impatiently crave more friends or memories – you're content with the ones you have, and this attitude is what makes us happy in the long term.

Does it mean that making money makes no sense, and we don't need it for happiness? Not at all. Few people can live in today's world without money (and I don't see you joining an indigenous tribe anytime soon to achieve this goal). Many experiences still cost money, and you can't buy them with a positive attitude alone. However, we generally overestimate how much we really need to make our wildest dreams come true.

A good example is Colin Wright, a blogger, speaker, and publisher who lives, for many, a dream lifestyle by traveling full-time[xxiv]. He only needs $30,000 to support this way of living, which is an immensely smaller amount than most of us would believe to be enough to travel the world perpetually.

Simplifying your life by getting rid of the clutter can help you save a lot of money that you can put into your "lifestyle experience" fund. Spend it wisely on living your life rather than hoarding stuff you can't take with you anyway.

WHAT REALLY MAKES YOU HAPPY: QUICK RECAP

1. Experiential purchases are more pleasurable and satisfying than material purchases. We tend to anticipate an experience with joy, while waiting for a material purchase makes us anxious. Moreover, we're more likely to reminisce about a great experience than an item.

2. Some people are hoarders. When they are confronted with throwing out their unnecessary stuff they experience deep pain and discomfort. A technique called "surfing the urge" can help you deal with this problem. The whole idea behind this method is being mindful of your feelings and letting them run their course before resuming your process of decluttering.

3. Getting rid of the clothes you no longer wear is the first, easiest step to declutter your life. By cleaning out your wardrobe, you'll experience the first taste of freedom from stuff. It's only when you physically throw out junk that you experience how liberating it can be.

4. Simplifying your life is not about making yourself miserable for the sake of having fewer things. Throw away what you don't need and keep things that are valuable to you. Don't try to fit a senseless mold of a "minimalist" owning just 100 things or less. For most of us it's not practical or reasonable.

5. A life revolving around experiences rather than things will make you more content with what you already have. You'll stop comparing yourself to others and improve your well-being long-term instead of experiencing only a short-term boost of happiness. Contentment with what we have (instead of anxiety about what we don't have) is what makes us happy.

Chapter 3: Simple Rules for Simplification

Surprise – you can simplify your life in a very simple way. As I already mentioned in the introduction, sometimes it's just one thing that has a huge impact on the results. In the case of simplification, coming up with a list of your personal rules is such a "one thing."

In this chapter, we'll discuss some of the most effective rules you can introduce in your life to simplify it without necessarily having to modify every little habit.

Three Rules You Can Introduce in Your Life to Simplify It

Having a set of clear, defined rules will help you make better decisions more quickly. It will dramatically reduce complexity by always having an answer to some of the most common questions and situations arising in your everyday life. Here are three suggested rules:

1. Always choose quality

As the saying goes, "you can't afford buying cheap things." No matter what it is, quality always trumps price.

If you buy cheap shoes, nine times out of ten you'll have to throw them out after a few months or sooner. In the end, you'll spend more money regularly buying cheap shoes than buying one good pair of shoes that would serve you for years to come (and age beautifully).

If you're buying cheap food, what you save today on your groceries will be replaced by money spent on medication in the future.

Prioritizing quality is one of the ultimate ways to simplify your life. You won't need to buy so many new things, because each of your purchases will be of high-quality and last longer. You'll enjoy your social life more, because instead of chasing after new friends you'll be satisfied with the ones you have. You'll learn how to be content with what you have, because you'll actually have something high-quality to be content with.

Buying clothes has always given me anxiety, because I always wanted to buy things as cheap as possible. When I changed my approach and started buying fewer, but only more expensive and generally high-quality items, my anxiety disappeared. You can't go wrong if you buy clothes made by an established, expensive brand (well, it's a good rule of thumb, anyway).

Wearing expensive clothing (even if you only have a few pieces) can also help you increase the overall quality of your life. In an interesting article on his blog, Neil Patel wrote how spending $162,301.42 on clothes made him $692,500[xxv].

What appears to be the total opposite of living the philosophy of minimalism is actually a great example of how simplification can improve your life. People do judge others by looks, and you can use this behavior to your benefit by carefully choosing how you're going to make a first impression on them. And is there a better way to do it than with high-quality, classic pieces of clothing that perfectly fit you?

Make a conscious effort to always choose quality over price. If you can't afford the more expensive product, save money until you can. You'll be better off waiting than buying the cheaper product of a lower quality.

2. Go after results, forget about effort

The essence of the 80/20 Principle is to avoid wasting time on things that matter little. If you disassociate effort from reward, life will get much simpler.

There's one question I ask myself each time I want to achieve a new goal. It's taken from Richard Koch's (ingenious) book *Living the 80/20 Way*[xxvi]:

"What will give me a much better result

for a lot less energy?"

Is there anything you're working on right now that isn't generating results as quickly as you'd like? How can you simplify it so that you only focus on the one most effective thing?

Following this rule in your life will help you save a lot of time and energy on unnecessary things. The reason why so many people are so busy isn't because they're such great workers. It's because they do the hard work instead of doing the smart work.

In the end, if you buy something, do you care how many hours it took to manufacture it? Do you care how many hours it takes your accountant to file your tax report? Does it make any difference whether an author spent three years writing his new book versus finishing it in two months? As long as the quality remains the same, putting more effort is wasteful.

There's a myth that if you want to succeed in anything, you have to work on it non-stop, ideally 12 hours every single day for the next decade. In reality, you need much less time to become exceptional at something.

A study on top musicians, athletes, actors and chess players conducted by professor K. Anders Ericsson and his colleagues at Florida State University[xxvii] shows that elite performers typically practice in highly-focused sessions lasting no more than 90 minutes. These world-class performers also rarely practice for more than four and a half hours a day.

As Dr. Ericsson says, "To maximize gains from long-term practice, individuals must avoid exhaustion and must limit practice to an amount from which they can completely recover on a daily or weekly basis."

There are many great examples of people following this rule to live simple, yet highly successful lives.

Warren Buffet, one of the most successful investors in the world, wrote in his 1990 letter to the shareholders of Berkshire Hathaway Inc., "Lethargy bordering on sloth remains the cornerstone of our investment style"[xxviii].

Richard Koch, a British multimillionaire known for his books about the 80/20 Principle, is one of the most striking examples of how simplification can help you become successful.

When he retired at 40 and decided to spend the majority of his time living a simple life of writing, bicycling, and living in the sunniest parts of the world, he carefully selected several companies (his simple rules for investment are explained in his book *The Star Principle*[xxix]) in which he invested.

While an average angel investor (a person investing in business startups) is usually happy with 20% returns, Richard made between 5 and 53 times his original equity stakes (that's 500% to 5300% return), and his worst result was doubling his investment. Most hard-working investors are satisfied achieving his worst results.

Richard Branson, a British billionaire known for his brand Virgin, is yet another example of focusing on results instead of effort. Instead of running the company personally, he delegates all of the work to managers who are free to run the company as they want[xxx].

In exchange, Branson can live on his tropical island Necker and spend time with his family instead of being a stereotypical always-busy CEO who has sacrificed his life to the pursuit of wealth.

Simplification is the way to go for everyone – even if you're a highly-ambitious overachiever.

3. Follow a system

Breaking big goals into small, manageable chunks is simplification at its best. Instead of envisioning a long, arduous journey to achieve your goals, think only about the next step. Just like you can drive your car during the night and only see a small part of the road ahead of you, you can focus on the next small step and forget about the end goal. This lets you avoid getting overwhelmed by your big goal.

As James Clear, a writer and researcher on behavioral psychology, habit formation, and performance improvement writes in his article, "Forget About Setting Goals. Focus on This Instead"[xxxi], "Goals can provide direction and even push you forward in the short-term, but eventually a well-designed system will always win. Having a system is what matters. Committing to the process is what makes the difference."

It's easy to implement this advice in your own life. Instead of setting a goal to lose 20 pounds in the next three months, set a system that will take you there.

For instance, eat no more than 2000 calories every single day or add an hour of daily exercise. As long as you stick to your system and adjust it based on the results you're getting (losing weight, maintaining weight, gaining weight), you'll end up where you want to go.

It's easy to disregard the small tasks done daily, but when you consider their long-term effect, they add up to a big achievement.

Writing a novel of 100,000 words sounds like an extremely daunting task. Yet, writing 1,000 words a day (which doesn't take more than one to two hours a day), results in writing such a book in a mere 100 days, a little over three months.

How quickly can you develop your career as an author if you promise yourself to stick to such a simple system? There's no need for anything complicated here – you sit in a chair and write 1000 words every single day.

You can apply this rule to every single aspect of your life.

If you're looking for a new job, set a system to send at least 10 resumes every single day. Within a month, you'll have reached out to 300 potential employers, greatly increasing your chances of finding a new job.

If you lack friends, set a system to have a friendly conversation with at least one new stranger a day. That's 30 strangers a month, 365 strangers a year. Surely you'll befriend at least one of them.

If you want to learn a new language, set a system to practice it for an hour a day. As Benny Lewis, author of a popular language learning blog, *Fluent in 3 Months*, and the author of a book of the same title, says that if it is your first time learning a language, it will take you about 600 hours to become fluent in it.[xxxii]

That's 600 days of practice, so you can learn how to speak a foreign language fluently in less than two years. Suddenly the goal of learning a new language isn't so daunting, is it?

The Power of Rules

There are many more rules you can incorporate in your life to simplify it. This list is by no means an extensive one. We all have different ways of living, and your rules should reflect that.

The entire idea behind the concept of "rules to simplify your life" is to have a pre-set way of dealing with things.

If I have a rule to always buy quality, and I'm faced with a decision to choose between a cheaper product of lower quality and a more expensive one, I won't waste time comparing every single feature – I'll go after high quality.

If I have a rule to focus on the results and not the effort, I won't do things for the sake of doing them. I save a tremendous amount of time by being aware of my activities, so I don't have to say "I'm busy" for the sole reason that I can't discern between the results and effort.

If my rule says to focus on the small wins, I don't waste too much time and energy worrying about the end goal. As long as I keep doing my daily small task, I will eventually achieve my goal.

Come up with your own set of rules to eliminate guesswork and wasted energy making decisions that should be made with no thinking at all.

Note: I decided against including one of my most important personal rules here. Instead, I go more in-depth with it, explaining it in the bonus chapter after the epilogue.

SIMPLE RULES FOR
SIMPLIFICATION: QUICK RECAP

1. Coming up with a list of your personal simplification rules will help you save time when making decisions. It will also prevent you from making the wrong choices that will complicate your life.

2. When you always choose quality, you greatly simplify your life by surrounding yourself with high-quality products that might cost more, but last much longer. The same philosophy, when applied to other aspects of your life, will ensure that you focus on value instead of price.

3. If you focus on the effort you put into something, you're much less effective than a person who focuses on working smart. Each time you want to do a certain task, ask yourself how you can do it more quickly and with less energy. Otherwise, you're making your life more difficult and complicated by wasting time and energy you could spend on something else.

4. Big goals are overwhelming, complex, and scary. It doesn't mean you shouldn't set them, though. The key is to break your huge goals down into small daily actions. When you prioritize the small steps instead of the big, scary goal, you'll still achieve your goal, but with less worry and more control. All you need to do is keep doing the same task over and over and assess its effectiveness.

Chapter 4: Release Yourself from Unnecessary Time Commitments

We all have various time commitments in our lives – as employees and employers, as parents and children, as members of the local community, and as spouses. All of these roles can take up a lot of our time.

However, perhaps with the exception of our careers (as a Gallup study of the American workplace from 2010 through 2012 shows[xxxiii], 70% of Americans don't like their jobs), the obligations we have are rewarding.

Picking up your kids from school is a bonding experience. Helping your spouse find a new job brings you closer to each other. Helping your local community makes you feel you're a part of something bigger. These obligations – although some of them can be unnecessary – are, in general, a healthy part of our lives.

The bigger problem – the 20% that causes 80% of the loss of time – comes directly from within us. Obviously, we don't call these things "time commitments" even though they usually look like one. They're called "things we like to do," even when we're aware they reduce the quality of our lives.

Too Much TV

One of the primary examples is watching television. American Time Use Survey in 2014 shows that an average person age 15 or over watches TV for almost three hours a day[xxxiv]. A Nielsen report from 2009 shows that the average American watches over 5 hours of TV a day[xxxv]. No matter what the final average is, it's certainly at least a few hours a day spent on a low-value activity.

According to the studies conducted at the Harvard School of Public Health, watching too much television increases the risk of obesity by 23%[xxxvi]. Another study from the same institution shows that watching more than two hours of TV daily was linked to a higher risk of type 2 diabetes and heart disease[xxxvii]. Moreover, watching more than three hours of TV a day leads to an increased risk of premature death.

These are just two studies showing the most obvious effects of watching too much TV. There's also research on the increased violence in kids watching too much TV[xxxviii]. Television also affects how we see the world around us (as a big, scary place full of terrorists, violence, and money being the sole purpose of living).

Is watching TV the worst thing you can do in your life? Of course not. It's a way to spend leisure time, and there's nothing inherently wrong with watching movies a few times a week. The problem starts when you fill your mind with the negative content and it becomes your main way of spending free time.

It becomes an obligation to sit in front of the television every evening and watch the new episodes of ten different series you follow. You feel you just "have to" watch the new episode of your favorite reality show, even though it tests your tolerance for stupidity. You can't miss the evening news – and not really because you want to know what's happening in the world, but because you can't resist the violent imagery and alarmist information.

Can you really live a simple life if every single day you consume information that tells you that:

- the world is a scary place and you should never leave your home and explore the world?

- you won't be happy if you don't buy the latest widget?

- the world revolves around money, and ethics are no longer important?

What if instead of filling your mind with these negative messages you turned off your TV and ventured outside? What if instead of believing what the TV is saying about other countries, you traveled there yourself and saw how things really are?

I used to hear about how dangerous it is to go to Mexico. Media loves to exaggerate bad news and describe the entire country by what's happening in one region of it.

When I went to Mexico to see it with my own eyes, I discovered one of the most peaceful places in the world. It wasn't violent at all. Actually, it was pretty boring. Granted, I didn't explore the (few) truly dangerous areas, and I don't ask you to. Still, the experience taught me that you can't judge a country by what you've heard on the news.

How about not having enough time to achieve your goals – isn't watching TV for a few hours a day an obstacle here? Plenty of people like to complain how busy they are and how little time they have to learn a new language, acquire a new skill, or practice a sport. Then they sit in front of the TV and waste hours on mindless entertainment.

Watching TV is one of the most common unnecessary time commitments. It adds little value in your life, and sucks a lot of time and energy you could spend on something else. While it's not your ultimate enemy if you want to simplify your life, it does negatively affect your well-being.

Too Much Social Media

Studies from Pew Research Center show that 74% of all online adults use social networking sites. Almost everybody under the age of 50 – 89% for adults aged 18-29 and 82% for adults aged 30-49 – uses some kind of social media[xxxix].

A 2014 poll by GlobalWebIndex on 170,000 respondents[xl] shows that the Internet is starting to dominate our days. Among the respondents, total hours spent online via PCs, laptops, mobiles and tablets grew from 5.55 in 2012 to 6.15 hours in 2014. The usage of social media has climbed from a daily average of 1.61 to 1.72 hours.

1 hour and 43 minutes a day spent on keeping up with what our friends ate on a given day. Granted, not all of us do it, but even if we don't necessarily look at everything our friends post, it's still a significant obstacle on our way to simplify our lives.

Too much social media takes a lot of value out of our daily experiences. I have a friend who's constantly on Facebook. If I go out with him, sometimes I can't enjoy a normal conversation because each time his phone blips, he has to check who messaged him and reply right away. You'd say he has bad manners (and it's probably true), but he says he simply can't resist it. And he's not alone.

I was dumbstruck when I once saw a group of five teenagers sitting at the same table in a fast food restaurant, each with a phone in her hand. They were with each other only physically – all of them were busy tapping something on their phones. How's the quality of their social interactions? Are they even able to go out with their friends and actually interact with them in person instead of online?

Social media has its place in your life. It can help you catch up with friends (particularly the ones who don't live in your city), get to know new people, and explore new things. However, when it starts to become one of your time commitments – you just can't stop checking your profile, even when you're outside with friends – something is wrong. Your life is no longer simple – it's dominated by distraction and anxiety.

Being connected all the time is surely great for your friends addicted to social media. They can always reach you and you always reply within seconds. It's not that great for your sanity, though. You stop paying attention to the world around you.

You live in constant anxiety, waiting for that rewarding sound of a new message.

Once when I was outside with my social media addicted friend, we watched the sunset. Instead of just enjoying the view, he pulled out his phone, took a photo and sent it to another person. It sounds like a bad joke, yet I'm pretty sure that he's not alone in seeing the sunset mostly behind his phone camera.

Solution – don't use social media on your phone. Access it only when you're at home, on your laptop or tablet. If it's something urgent, you'll get a call. If it's not urgent, enjoy being outside instead of giving half of your attention to your friend physically with you and another half to your other friend who's online.

Saying Yes to Energy Vampires

We all know these people. You get depressed, annoyed, frustrated, bored, or stressed after spending just a few minutes with these people. Even though you know they're bad company for you, sometimes it's hard to cut ties with them – after all, you've known them for years.

Yet, that's precisely what you should do, the sooner, the better. Some people just can't be helped. The only result of spending time with them is more negative emotions for you. What's the point?

The entire premise behind simplification is to enjoy your life more by getting rid of what's not working for you – things that are unnecessary or simply a bad fit. Negative people are always a bad fit, and it's not just a waste of time to hang out with them.

Neuroscience shows that listening to people who complain damages your brain. Robert Sapolsky at Stanford University's School of Medicine says that listening to someone whining or gossiping elevates cortisol levels. This, in turn, makes a part of your brain called the hippocampus shrink. As a result, it leads to a decline in cognitive function, including the ability to solve problems, retain information, and adapt to new situations[xli].

The 80/20 Principle applies to relationships in exactly the same way as getting rid of your stuff. 80% of your enjoyment comes out of 20% of the relationships. And 80% of unhappiness in relationships comes from 20% of your friends. Who are they?

How often do you spend time with people who you don't particularly like just because you think you should keep seeing them? How much value does it provide in your life? Wouldn't it be better to spend this time with friends who you like more?

RELEASE YOURSELF FROM UNNECESSARY TIME COMMITMENTS: QUICK RECAP

1. Watching television makes your life more complicated by making you lazier and increasing your risk of many health disorders. It provides little value in your life while taking away a lot. A person who gets her information from TV is constantly bombarded with the "consume more" message, which makes it difficult to resist the temptation to buy new things for the sake of feeling better.

2. Using too much social media is a sure-fire way to lead a distracted life. If you're constantly connected, it's easy to overlook and miss enjoying the little things in life that matter a lot – a beautiful sunset, a stranger's smile, or simply the feeling of sitting alone in the woods or on the beach. Consider getting rid of social media on your phone and giving your full attention to the world around you whenever you leave your home.

3. Spending time with energy vampires for the sake of catching up is another common unnecessary

time commitment. You have no obligation to keep spending time with people you no longer like. If a social interaction with someone is not making you happy, consider cutting ties with this person. Free up time for more positive friends.

Chapter 5: Life Is Simpler for the Positive Mind

The world around you can make your life more difficult and complicated. Oftentimes, though, most of the problems originate from your mind and attitude.

How often do you worry? How often do you complain? How often do you speak badly about others and send off negative vibes?

All of these things – and other common behaviors of pessimistic people – complicate your life. In fact, most problems start with the wrong attitude. No matter what happens to you, the interpretation is made by you and shapes your entire life.

For one person, a problem at work is a disaster, for another it's a challenge. For one person, reading books and educating herself is a waste of time, for another (humble) person, books are the source of knowledge she applies in her life to grow.

A person who is content with what she has exhibits a positive attitude, being grateful for what she has. A person with a negative mindset focuses on what she lacks, thus constantly trying to fill the void with stuff, thinking it will finally help her become happy (sorry, won't happen).

How can you develop a positive mind to make your life simpler? In this chapter, we'll discuss the key aspects of living a happy and positive life, and how it can cut away a lot of junk from your life.

Three Essential Steps to Have a Positive Mindset

There are three crucial steps you need to take in order to become a positive person. By saying no to further negativity and focusing on the bright side of life, you'll get rid of many problems (quite a few of which are created entirely by you). The first step to develop a positive mind starts with…

1. Gratitude

All positive psychology experts agree that expressing gratitude is the key to a happy and positive life. There are so many interesting benefits of gratitude that it's worth covering them in detail.

A 2014 study on gratitude and economic impatience (instant gratification vs delayed gratification) developed by David DeSteno from Northeastern University in Boston, MA shows that gratitude reduces impatience[xlii]. Thus, it can help you make better financial decisions, which in turn will reduce the number of financial problems in your life.

Another study, conducted by the researchers from the University of New South Wales in Australia shows that saying thank you to new acquaintances makes them more likely to become your friend[xliii]. Sounds obvious, yet how often do we forget that such simple gestures have such a powerful effect on our social interactions? In this case, one little thing can help you develop new high-quality friendships – a vital thing from a trivial little action.

According to a 2012 analysis on 1,000 Swiss adults, people who are grateful report feeling healthier than other people[xliv]. They experience fewer aches and pains, are more likely to exercise, and do regular medical check-ups. A 2011 study on gratitude and sleep shows that expressing gratitude before bed improves sleep[xlv]. Yet again, being grateful can lead to powerful benefits. Nothing is more important than health, and expressing gratitude has been proven to improve both your physical and mental health.

Robert A. Emmons, the world's leading scientific expert on gratitude at the University of California, Davis, has conducted numerous studies[xlvi] that show how powerful gratitude is to reduce depression, improve happiness, and lead to what we call "a good life." In addition, a study conducted by a team led by C. Nathan DeWall at the University of Kentucky shows that gratitude reduces aggression and enhances empathy[xlvii].

There are also studies showing that gratitude increases athlete's self-esteem (which leads to improved performance)[xlviii] and that it can help deal with negative body image and anxiety disorder[xlix]. It can also help overcome trauma[l] and foster resilience[li].

There's something extremely powerful in making yourself aware of how many things you take for granted. Gratitude is a perfect example of a how one small thing can lead to extremely powerful changes in everyday life. If you wish to live a simpler and happier life, thankfulness is a must.

The simplest way to introduce gratitude in your life is to start each day by expressing your gratitude for three to five things in your life. There's no need to come up with extraordinary things – a smile on your spouse's face, a success at work, a sunny day outside are all valid reasons to be grateful. If you enjoy journaling, consider starting your own gratitude journal so you can jot down things for which you are thankful.

This one simple habit is an important 20% activity leading to 80% of the results. Even if you disregard the rest of the advice from this chapter, you'll still change your life for the better.

2. Resilience

If gratitude is the number one thing to live a happy life, resilience has to be the second most important factor. People who are resilient don't tend to stay depressed for a long time. They know how to deal with setbacks, failure, and insurmountable obstacles. Trauma, while it does affect them like everyone else, can't destroy their spirit.

Thankfully (see what I did there?), resilience is a skill everyone can learn. There are numerous ways to build your resilience. The American Psychological Association suggests 10 tips such as maintaining good relationships with close family members and friends, accepting circumstances that can't be changed, and keeping things in perspective[lii].

Sonja Lyubomirsky and Matthew Della Porta at the University of Riverside, California suggest in their paper about happiness and resilience[liii] that the best way to enhance resilience is to focus on experiencing more positive emotions, thoughts and events in your life. Joy and satisfaction counteract the negative effects of trauma and stress, making you more resilient.

It all ties together so well. Focus on simplifying your life to make more room for high-quality experiences, people and emotions. As a reward, you not only live a happier life, but also develop more resilience to deal with negative events better. In the end, you achieve long-term happiness and the ability to stay positive even when bad things happen in your life.

3. Problem-solving skills

Worrying puts you into an unproductive state of mind that, instead of helping you come up with solutions, makes you enter a vicious cycle of negative thoughts. Worrying is never useful and is one of the many trivial activities that contributes to unhappiness in your life.

You worry about something that can happen. If it happens, it reinforces your habit to worry. If it doesn't happen, you're still going to worry about something else because you haven't developed the proper way to deal with worrying.

Problem-solving skills will help you reduce your worrying to a minimum. Dale Carnegie suggests in his classic book, *How to Stop Worrying and Start Living*[liv], four steps to stop worrying:

1. Writing down precisely what I am worried about.

2. Writing down what I can do about it.

3. Deciding what to do.

4. Starting immediately to carry out that decision.

Exhibiting this behavior – instead of spending time worrying – will lead you to a happier and easier life. It's also simpler to sit down with a problem and solve it rather than spend hours worrying about the eventual outcome.

LIFE IS SIMPLER FOR THE POSITIVE MIND: QUICK RECAP

1. You can't live a simple, satisfying life without exhibiting a positive attitude toward the world. Negative emotions lead people to the wrong kind of sources of happiness. A person who constantly complains and isn't grateful for what she has will always think there's something lacking in her life, thus constantly buying new things for the short-term, empty feeling of reward.

2. Gratitude is the most crucial emotion you should cultivate in your life to be positive and happy. Various studies show that it helps you make better financial decisions, make friends, improve your physical and mental health, reduce aggression, enhance empathy, boost self-esteem, and deal with stress and trauma. Gratitude is a perfect example of a little thing leading to big results.

3. Resilience is a necessary skill for everyone who wishes to experience long-term happiness. If you can't handle problems and bad events in life, it will be difficult to cultivate a positive mindset.

Thankfully, expressing gratitude and allowing other positive emotions in your life will help you improve your ability to deal with and bounce back from setbacks, failure, and negative events.

4. Worrying is a useless activity that produces no value, yet takes away a lot of energy. Instead of worrying, incorporate a habit of coming up with potential solutions, picking the best one, and acting on it. Spending any amount of time with worry is wasteful and makes you unproductive.

Epilogue

Achieving simplicity in life is a process, not an event. In the five chapters of this book, I intended to discuss with you some of the ways you can simplify your life.

What works for me doesn't necessarily work for you. Consider this book an invitation to explore the world of simplicity on your own. Try a few of the ideas described here and see if they work for you.

As long as you stick to the general rule – get more with less – you will certainly make your life simpler and more enjoyable. It doesn't mean you have to force yourself to live with 100 things, try to stretch your money, or avoid getting a job with more responsibilities.

Simplicity is about making things simpler, but nothing more drastic than that.

As with all of my books, this book is an 80/20 book – an overview of the topic with numerous references and scientific studies. I strongly urge you to dig deeper by reading:

Essentialism by Greg McKeown – a brilliant book if you want to get rid of the unessential things to make room for what really matters.

Living the 80/20 Way by Richard Koch – probably the best book ever written about the 80/20 Principle. It provides numerous exercises that will help you implement the rule in your life and make it simpler.

The ONE Thing by Gary Keller – a good way to describe this book would be to say it's a guide for achievers who like to keep things simple. Gary takes the 80/20 Principle to the next level.

These three books will surely point you in the right direction and help you immerse yourself in a wonderful world where effort and quantity doesn't matter. What matters instead is getting the results you're after – whether it's more happiness, achievement, order, love, or success.

I sincerely hope my book becomes a spark to make changes in your life. Life is so much more pleasant and easier when you focus on what's important and disregard the rest.

Bonus Chapter: A Simple Life Needs No Lies

Warning: many claims in this chapter won't have a scientific backing. Unlike the other chapters in this book, this section is more philosophical. However, it still offers practical advice to implement right away in your life. Since it's different than all the previous chapters in this book, I'm adding it as a bonus chapter.

When someone lies a lot, we tend to say this person is "entangled in a web of her lies." A white lie often leads to a few more, equally "harmless" lies that quickly take on their own life, thus making the web of lies more and more tangled.

How do you expect to live a simple life if you have to constantly ask yourself whether you've lied to someone or told her the truth?

Lying is one of the ultimate ways to complicate your life. It's not only a burden on your conscience, but, as studies show, also your health. A study conducted by Anita E. Kelly and Lijuan Wang at the university of Notre Dame[lv] shows that lying less is linked to better health. Moreover, fewer lies lead to the improvement of close personal relationships and social interactions in general.

Yet, evidence cited in the same study shows that Americans average about 11 lies per week. Life could be so much simpler for them if they only stopped lying.

How to Simplify Your Life by Not Lying

If you're seeking a simpler life, consider adopting honesty as one of your most important personal values. In the rest of this chapter, we'll discuss the most common reasons why people lie, how it complicates their lives, and how honesty can help these individuals avoid problems.

The first, and probably most common, reason why people lie is out of "kindness." You don't tell your friend she doesn't look good in a new dress. When someone asks you if he's fat, you say that he's perfect (even if he's morbidly obese). You don't want to reject someone, so instead of simply saying "no," you say you're "busy" and keep delaying, hoping the other person gives up before you're forced to say what you really think.

Now, you don't have to agree with me regarding what a white lie is and whether it's ethical to speak one or not. Everything I'm saying – as everything in this book – is a suggestion, a possible change you can make in your life to benefit from more simplicity.

Let's look at these innocent white lies in a long-term perspective. Nine times out of ten, when someone asks you for an honest opinion that's exactly what she wants – an honest opinion. When (and not if), this person finds out you usually lie to please her, guess what... She will never trust your opinion again, or at least think twice before believing you. Is this a solid foundation for a relationship? I don't think so.

Let's examine the next situation – an obese friend is concerned about his weight. You, instead of pointing out in a polite way his worries are indeed well-founded, say "no, you're perfect."

A year or two passes, and your friend gets more and more obese. His health deteriorates, and he can no longer enjoy certain activities due to a low level of fitness. While your white lie was definitely not the only reason why this person remained obese, don't you think an honest opinion of a close friend wouldn't at least ignite a spark of interest in the subject of losing weight?

In the last scenario – instead of straight out rejecting a person telling her to "call later" – you complicate your life on a daily basis. A simple rejection cuts short any unwelcome invitations.

If your colleague asks you for a date and you reject him, he'll stop his advances (or at least, a gentleman would). If you keep trying to be nice by offering a white lie ("I'm so terribly busy now, maybe next month"), you're guaranteeing this person will keep asking you out until he either gives up or you finally get honest with him (and make him bitter for misleading him for so long).

In all three cases, an innocent white lie only complicates your life by generating new problems. Telling the truth can be painful and uncomfortable in the short term, but it saves you (and other people) pain and discomfort later on.

A second common reason why people lie is because they want to achieve a certain goal with no regard for consequences. This form of lying is extremely common among men, some of whom would do anything to charm their way into a woman's bed. Women, in return, are often forced to play the same game of manipulation – otherwise they'll fall victim to a dishonest, Machiavellian character.

A straight-shooter doesn't play games. You can't game him, and he won't game you.

Wouldn't life be simpler for you as a woman (or a homosexual man) if a man interested in you sexually would state his intention from the beginning instead of pretending to want to be only your friend? It would be your choice to decide whether you want to continue your conversation with him or not. No matter your decision, at least you wouldn't have to wonder whether someone's intentions are clear or not.

Wouldn't life be simpler for you as a man (or a homosexual woman) if you clearly stated you're seeking a woman's companionship because you're interested in her romantically or sexually?

It doesn't mean you have to be impolite or too upfront. A simple decision to stop lying about your intention to be someone's friend (when you're not interested in friendship at all) would greatly simplify your life.

When a woman says she's taken, you wouldn't say, "It's okay, I only want to be your friend," and then wonder why you're in the friend zone. You would simply move on, thus only spending your time with people who share your intentions.

A great book explaining how being upfront and straightforward in your romantic life can simplify it is Alan Roger Currie's book, *MODE ONE: Let The Women Know What You're REALLY Thinking* (it's interesting and useful for both men and women).

A third common reason why people lie is because they want to make themselves look better than they really are. This type of a lie has an obvious source – a lack of self-esteem. Would you need to lie if you knew for a fact you're a valuable, interesting human being?

In this case, lying complicates your life by covering the essence of the problem. It's like putting a Band-Aid on an open wound. If you want it to heal quickly, you don't cover it – you sew it shut.

In the case of lying to make yourself appear more interesting, you're covering the fact you lack a belief in your worth. How does it serve you in life? Isn't it more difficult to try to appear to be an interesting person than to simply become one?

Lying has no place in your life if you wish to simplify it. Start today by telling the truth instead of telling white lies or using lies for short-term gratification.

A SIMPLE LIFE NEEDS NO LIES: QUICK RECAP

1. Lying is a burden on your conscience and your health. If you wish to live a simpler, happier life, stop lying.

2. People lie for a wide variety of reasons, but each motivation usually prioritizes short-term gratification over the long-term consequences. Would you rather experience some discomfort now and have a clear conscience, or save yourself discomfort now in exchange for huge negative consequences in the future? That's the choice you're making each time you're deciding whether to lie or tell the truth.

3. Lying can cover the underlying reasons why you lie, thus making it more difficult to become more critical of yourself and fix what's broken. If you lie because you want to make yourself look like a better person, perhaps your self-esteem needs fixing. Lying won't solve your problem.

Download another Book for Free

I want to thank you for buying my book and offer you another book (just as valuable as this book), *Grit: How to Keep Going When You Want to Give Up*, completely free.

Visit the link below to receive it:

http://www.profoundselfimprovement.com/purea ndsimple

In *Grit*, I'll share with you exactly how to stick to your goals according to peak performers and science.

In addition to getting *Grit*, you'll also have an opportunity to get my new books for free, enter giveaways and receive other valuable emails from me.

Again, here's the link to sign up:

http://www.profoundselfimprovement.com/purea ndsimple

Could You Help?

I'd love to hear your opinion about my book. In the world of book publishing, there are few things more valuable than honest reviews from a wide variety of readers.

Your review will help other readers find out whether my book is for them. It will also help me reach more readers by increasing the visibility of my book.

About Martin Meadows

Martin Meadows is the pen name of an author who has dedicated his life to personal growth. He constantly reinvents himself by making drastic changes in his life.

Over the years, he has regularly fasted for over 40 hours, taught himself two foreign languages, lost over 30 pounds in 12 weeks, ran several businesses in various industries, took ice-cold showers and baths, lived on a small tropical island in a foreign country for several months, and wrote a 400-page long novel's worth of short stories in one month.

Yet, self-torture is not his passion. Martin likes to test his boundaries to discover how far his comfort zone goes.

His findings (based both on his personal experience and scientific studies) help him improve his life. If you're interested in pushing your limits and learning how to become the best version of yourself, you'll love Martin's works.

You can read his books here:

http://www.amazon.com/author/martinmeadows.

---

[i] Koch R., *The 80/20 Principle: The Secret to Achieving More with Less*, 1997.

[ii] Iyengar S. S., Lepper M. R., "When choice is demotivating: can one desire too much of a good thing?" *Journal of Personality and Social Psychology* 2000; 79 (6): 995–1006.

[iii] Thompson D. V., Hamilton R. W., Rust R. T., "Feature Fatigue: When Product Capabilities Become Too Much of a Good Thing." *Journal of Marketing Research* 2005; 42 (4): 431–442.

[iv] Iyengar S.S., Huberman G., Jiang W. "How much choice is too much? Contributions to 401 (k) retirement plans." *Pension Research Council Working Paper* 2003.

[v] http://www.vanityfair.com/politics/2012/10/michael-lewis-profile-barack-obama, Web. June 28th, 2015.

[vi] http://elitedaily.com/money/science-simplicity-successful-people-wear-thing-every-day/849141/, Web. June 28th, 2015.

[vii] http://www.smh.com.au/entertainment/tv-and-radio/karl-stefanovics-sexism-experiment-today-presenter-wears-same-suit-for-a-year-20141115-11ncdz.html, Web. June 28th, 2015.

[viii] http://rippedbody.jp/the-big-3-routine/, Web. June 28th, 2015.

[ix] Dunbar R. I. M., "Neocortex size as a constraint on group size in primates." *Journal of Human Evolution* 1992; 22 (6): 469–493.

[x] http://spectrum.ieee.org/telecom/internet/how-many-friends-can-you-really-have, Web. June 29th, 2015.

[xi] King S., *On Writing. A Memoir of the Craft*, 2000.

[xii] http://www.entrepreneur.com/article/219988, Web. June 29th, 2015.

[xiii] Kumar A., Killingsworth M. A., Gilovich T. "Waiting for Merlot Anticipatory Consumption of Experiential and Material Purchases." *Psychological Science* 2014; 25 (10): 1924–1931.

[xiv] Van Boven L., Gilovich T. "To Do or to Have? That Is the Question." *Journal of Personality and Social Psychology* 2003; 85 (6): 1193–1202.

[xv] Van Boven L. "Experientialism, Materialism, and the Pursuit of Happiness." *Review of General Psychology* 2005; 9 (2): 132–142.

[xvi] Solnick S. J., Hemenway D. "Is more always better?: A survey on positional concerns." *Journal of Economic Behavior & Organization* 1998; 37: 373–383.

[xvii] Tolin D. F. et al. "Neural mechanisms of decision making in hoarding disorder." *Archives of General Psychiatry* 2012; 69: 832–841.

[xviii] Bowen S., Marlatt A. "Surfing the urge: brief mindfulness-based intervention for college student smokers." Psychology of Addictive Behaviors 2009; 23 (4): 666–671.

[xix] You can learn more about mindfulness in: Hanh T. N., The Miracle of Mindfulness, 1975.

[xx] Vohs K. D., Redden J. P., Rahinel R. "Physical order produces healthy choices, generosity, and conventionality, whereas disorder produces creativity." *Psychological Science* 2013; 24 (9): 1860–1867.

[xxi] Pchelin P., Howell R. T. "The Hidden Cost of Value-seeking: People do not Accurately Forecast the Economic Benefits of Experiential Purchases." *The Journal of Positive Psychology* 2014; 9 (4): 322–334.

[xxii] Ruvio A., Somer E., Rindfleisch A. "When bad gets worse: the amplifying effect of materialism on traumatic stress and maladaptive consumption." *Journal of the Academy of Marketing Science* 2014; 42 (1): 90–101.

[xxiii] http://www.nytimes.com/2006/02/08/health/08iht-snmat.html?_r=0, Web., July 6th, 2015.

[xxiv] http://www.forbes.com/sites/laurashin/2015/07/02/how-this-30-year-old-travels-the-world-on-as-little-as-30000-a-year/, Web., July 6th, 2015.

[xxv] http://www.quicksprout.com/2014/12/10/how-spending-162301-42-on-clothes-made-me-692500/, Web., July 8th, 2015.

[xxvi] Koch R., *Living the 80/20 Way: Work Less, Worry Less, Succeed More, Enjoy More*, 2004.

[xxvii] http://www.nytimes.com/2013/02/10/opinion/sunday/relax-youll-be-more-productive.html?pagewanted=all, Web. February 26th, 2015.

xxviii http://www.berkshirehathaway.com/letters/1990.html, Web., July 9th, 2015.

xxix Koch R., The Star Principle: How It Can Make You Rich, 2008.

xxx http://www.entrepreneur.com/article/219988, Web. July 9th, 2015.

xxxi http://jamesclear.com/goals-systems, Web. July 9th, 2015.

xxxii http://www.fluentin3months.com/hours-to-learn-a-language/, Web., July 9th, 2015.

xxxiii http://www.gallup.com/services/178514/state-american-workplace.aspx, Web., July 10th, 2015.

xxxiv http://www.bls.gov/news.release/atus.nr0.htm, Web. July 10th, 2015.

xxxv

http://www.nielsen.com/us/en/insights/news/2009/americans-watching-more-tv-than-ever.html, Web. July 10th, 2015.

xxxvi Hu F. B., Li T. Y., Colditz G. A., Willett W. C., Manson J. E. "Television watching and other sedentary behaviors in relation to risk of obesity and type 2 diabetes mellitus in women." *Journal of the American Medical Association* 2003; 289 (14): 1785–1791.

xxxvii Grøntved A., Hu F. B. "Television Viewing and Risk of Type 2 Diabetes, Cardiovascular Disease, and All-Cause Mortality: A Meta-analysis." *Journal of the American Medical Association* 2011; 305 (23): 2448–2455.

xxxviii Robertson L. A., McAnally H. M., Hancox R. J. "Childhood and Adolescent Television Viewing and Antisocial Behavior in Early Adulthood." *Pediatrics* 2013, February 18.

xxxix http://www.pewinternet.org/data-trend/social-media/social-media-use-by-age-group/, Web., July 12th, 2015.

xl https://www.globalwebindex.net/blog/daily-time-spent-on-social-networks-rises-to-1-72-hours, Web. July 12th, 2015.

xli Described in: Blake T., *Three Simple Steps: A Map to Success in Business and Life*, 2012. Also mentioned in my book *Grit: How to Keep Going When You Want to Give Up*.

xlii DeSteno D., Li Y., Dickens L., Lerner J. S., "Gratitude A Tool for Reducing Economic Impatience." *Psychological Science* 2014; 25 (6): 1262–1267.

xliii Williams L. A., Bartlett M. Y. "Warm Thanks: Gratitude Expression Facilitates Social Affiliation in New Relationships via Perceived Warmth." *Emotion* 2014; 15 (1): 1–5.

xliv Hill P. L., Allemand M., Roberts B. W. "Examining the Pathways between Gratitude and Self-Rated Physical Health across Adulthood." *Personality and Individual Differences* 2013; 54 (1): 92–96.

xlv Digdon N., Koble A. "Effects of Constructive Worry, Imagery Distraction, and Gratitude Interventions on Sleep Quality: A Pilot Trial." *Applied Psychology: Health and Well-Being* 2011; 3 (2): 193–206.

xlvi To name a few, see: Emmons R. A., McCullough M. E. "Counting Blessings Versus Burdens: An Experimental Investigation of Gratitude and Subjective Well-Being in Daily Life." *Journal of Personality and Social Psychology* 2003; 84 (2): 377–389; Emmons R. A., Crumpler C. A. "Gratitude as a Human Strength: Appraising the Evidence." *Journal of Social and Clinical Psychology* 2000; 19 (1): 56–69; Froh J. J., Sefick W. J., Emmons R. A. "Counting blessings in early adolescents: An experimental study of gratitude and subjective well-being." *Journal of School Psychology* 2008; 46 (2): 213–233.

xlvii DeWall C. N., Lambert N. M., Pond Jr. R. S., Kashdan T. B., Fincham, F. D. "A grateful heart is a non-violent heart: Cross-sectional, experience sampling, longitudinal, and experimental evidence." *Social Psychological and Personality Science* 2012; 3 (2): 232–240.

xlviii Chen L. H., Wu C. H. "Gratitude Enhances Change in Athletes' Self-Esteem: The Moderating Role of Trust in Coach." *Journal of Applied Sport Psychology* 2014; 26 (3): 349–362..

xlix Wood A. M., Froh J. J., Geraghty A. W. "Gratitude and well-being: a review and theoretical integration." *Clinical Psychology Review* 2010; 30 (7): 890–905.

[l] Kashdan T. B., Uswatte G., Julian T. "Gratitude and hedonic and eudaimonic well-being in Vietnam war veterans." *Behaviour Research and Therapy* 2006; 44: 177–199.

[li] Fredrickson B. L., Tugade M. M., Waugh C. E., Larkin G. R. "What Good Are Positive Emotions in Crises? A Prospective Study of Resilience and Emotions Following the Terrorist Attacks on the United States on September 11th, 2001." *Journal of Personality and Social Psychology* 2003; 84 (2): 365–376.

[lii] Read the full article on resilience for a broader view of the subject: http://www.apa.org/helpcenter/road-resilience.aspx, Web. July 13th, 2015.

[liii] Lyubomirsky S., Della Porta M. D. 'Boosting happiness, buttressing resilience: Results from cognitive and behavioral interventions." In: Reich J. W., Zautra A. J., Hall J. S., editors. *Handbook of adult resilience*, Guilford Press; *New York* 2010. pp. 450–464.

[liv] Carnegie D., *How to Stop Worrying and Start Living*, Pocket Books; Revised edition 1990.

[lv] http://www.apa.org/news/press/releases/2012/08/lying-less.aspx, Web., July 7th, 2015.

Printed in Great Britain
by Amazon

21342128R00058